# Inside What Door

## Is Your

# Marriage In?

## Eight Short Stories

ARACELIS MALDONADO

ISBN 978-1-0980-5583-7 (paperback)
ISBN 978-1-0980-5584-4 (digital)

Christian Faith Publishing, Inc.
832 Park Avenue
Meadville, PA 16335
www.christianfaithpublishing.com

Printed in the United States of America

To my children, Elias, Jennifer, and Priscilla. When I needed my children the most, all of you were there for me.

To my daughter-in-law Sabrina, thank you for sharing verses with me from the Bible to uplift my spirit.

To Rev. Edgar and his wife, Mayda. I thank them from the bottom of my heart in staying with me through this journey.

# Introduction

When Moses was in front of the sea, God asked him, "What do you have in your hands?" I want to let you know that God asked me the same question. God then told me that it was my book that was in my hands. Amen.

But in all, I want to give God the glory because it is about him. And because of him, he took me out of my brokenness and used it for his glory. I love you, Lord.

To my readers, may my story be a blessing in your marriage. As you read my prayers and see how I cried out to the Lord, may it uplift you to want to do the same in your marriage. Never give up on your marriage. Never give up on God.

For the readers to know, I was praying and fasting before this storm happened in my life. This is my prayer on this day: Lord, I ask you in the name of Jesus, restore my marriage, heal and touch my husband from the top of his head to the sole of his feet. Make him new again that he finds joy again in you and love that he knows that he is your child. Devil, you don't have a place in this marriage or in our lives. Lord, I trust in you. I will worship you no matter what. I ask that you restore our lives.

At the church where I attend, the pastor's message is about living a life of peace. How familiar are you in life with stress? We haven't learned how to deal with stress. God, heal my marriage. "A heart at peace gives life to the body, but envy rots the bones" (Proverbs 14:30).

Thank you, Lord, for being in my life and answering my prayers. Lord, you know my heart and the negative out of my marriage. Peace and a new day is what I ask you in Jesus's name for healing in my marriage.

# Prophecy from the Lord

This prophecy was used by Rev. Edgar Rivera: covenant in my marriage, global protection in Jesus's name, a new covenant in my marriage. Jesus is protecting my marriage and getting married again. A global protection from the Lord means that *nothing can harm us*. He healed my husband, making him new again. No more blood pressure, he is a new man in Christ.

1. Receive your husband.
2. "Receive it," says the Lord.
3. God's promises.
4. Financial promises.
5. Working for Christ.
6. My husband's singing getting a lot of blessings.

"Sule, I see you receiving a lot of gifts," said Rev. Edgar Rivera.

I said, "My wonderful God is real in my heart and in my life."

I woke up in the morning. I prayed and walked to the beach, meditating with the Lord on how he showed me how all the birds flying low on sea as a reminder of how I will walk with my husband, Holy Spirit, and family. Awesome God, what an awesome God.

I was visiting Rev. Edgar Rivera in the church that he attends. The pastor preached, "Turn around to make a change. Today is a day to make a change. Deal with so many hurts."

"Now all glory to God, who is able, through his mighty power at work within us, to accomplish infinitely more than we might ask or think" (Ephesians 3:20).

Pastor preached, "Bankruptcy takes your health. Bankruptcy spiritually separates you slowly from the Lord and keeps you away from God gradually and slowly." God keeps reminding me to *be still*. Thank you, Lord, for reminding me to continuously focus on you and not on my situation. God gives me strength to stand, and he is doing more than I could ever imagine.

I just began to sing to the Lord to restore my joy and peace. I tell the Lord that I wait on him, and I need his strength. I thank God and thank him to be with me every morning and teach me how to love him more and more. Thank you, Lord. Thank you for speaking to me, and I am thankful to walk with Jesus. Throughout this day, I am trusting in you, Lord. We need to be grateful even when we are going through trials. I am walking through this valley, but at the end, I have the victory in Jesus's name. God is powerful. God is righteous. God is my helper, my healer. God is the same today, yesterday, and forever. He will never leave nor forsake me.

## A Vision from God Using Rev. Edgar Rivera

He's in control. "If he leaves, cry out," says the Lord. Speak to the Lord. Trust the Lord. He's in control. God's covering me with new love. He is dwelling in the past, and I am going into the new future. God is going to bring him out and into the new future—new life heading to the promised land in Jesus's name. God is in control.

To my daughter, he is in control. God is going to give you favor.

Rev. Edgar Rivera and I prayed for a baby who was seven months old that has a condition with his eyes. We prayed healing from the top of his head to the bottom of his feet in Jesus's name. Amen.

## My Prayer to the Lord

"Lord, you know how much I love my husband. I've been committed to him faithfully even though he had forgotten me a long time ago. I was still there. My love for him is still there, but I am done, no more hurting. Lord, I want my husband to be a new man in Christ and that he loves you first and then give him back to me, Lord. Let it be your will in Jesus's name. Amen.

I was praying in the morning, and God reminded me about Lazarus and how he raised him from the dead. God reminded me he can raise my situation.

## A Vision from the Lord Using Rev. Edgar Rivera

My husband walked back to the cross and confessed his sins in Jesus's name. Amen. Stay firm with the Lord. I am walking through the storm, keeping me firm with Christ right next to me. God is with me and giving me the promised land. Amen. Nothing can move me today, standing firm with the Lord.

## A Word from God

I am investing in the Lord, and I am getting an increase in the Lord and a better life. Walking with assurance, God is favoring you in the Lord. Rev. Edgar was up by 5:00 a.m., and the Lord told him to pray for Sule and her husband because the time has come. It was told to me that my husband was not investing in the Lord and only living a sinful nature. When you choose, choose God's kingdom only, and when you don't, bad investments arise and come into your life—no peace, no good health, no joy, and many worldly things. I began meditating on the Lord.

I was talking to a dear friend of mine, and she stated, "You have a testimony, and your story is not finished yet." I began speaking to the Lord, "Lord, please, I know the promises you have for me. I want you to tell me what is going on with my husband because I want to know so I can move forward. And let me know because he has never been honest with me. The worse feeling is being taken for granted. It is wrong, Lord, and I want to be completely done with all of this, but my heart is so broken.

"Help me, Lord, to become stronger, and when I speak to him, I may say the right things. Open his eyes so that he can get right with you. I get angry at times, Lord, fighting this by myself, and I cannot communicate with anyone or my children. It is so hard, and I only talk to you, Lord. Help me because I cannot take this anymore. I am fifty-six years old, Lord. Who wants to go through this? This is not right. I am so fed up with it all. Oh my God, you are the only one that can help me, Lord.

"Lord, if I die, I want my children to know I love them and always pray for them. I know that they will always serve you, and I pray they seek you first. If I am gone today or tomorrow, I want my husband to know that I forgive him for all he had done to me. All the lies don't matter, and I love him with all my heart. Lord, if I did anything right, it was when I gave my heart to my husband. Make him understand that I feel so lonely and sad. I feel too much pain, and I wish I was not going through this, but I trust in you, Lord, always."

## A Word from Rev. Edgar Rivera

Showing the love of Christ to your worst enemy is not easy, but I am doing it through Christ the Lord. Remember when Jesus carried the cross and then he fell, a Roman soldier came to him and helped him get back up because he saw him tired. The Lord sees me tired and falling. Not every hero wears a cape. God was wearing the cross on his back. Jesus is my hero, and he is going to get me through it—my hurting, my loneliness. I'm keeping the faith. The Lord sees me constantly tired, but he will show me through it and reminds me daily to stay strong. Thank you, Lord.

Say the word, Father, and we are going to see the miracle in our lives. God's Word breathes on me. Oh Lord, breathe on me. Let your Holy Spirit breathe on me. Amen. The Lord reminded me of all my promises. I read through it again. Thank you, Lord. It was a reminder of who He is, God the creator, the beginning and the end.

Today's word from God is *victory*, *power*, and *peace*. Victory in Jesus, there is power in the name of Jesus. The Lord reminded me of the song "There Is Power in the Name of Jesus."

There was a vision from Rev. Edgar as we prayed. Jesus was walking through the light with Rev. Edgar, his wife, and I between my husband. God is the flashlight of my husband's direction. The Lord reminded Rev. Edgar and I of the song "Victory Is Mine."

In church, I was reminded that I'm no longer a slave to fear. I am a child of God. He opened the sea for you to walk through it, and you are going to have victory. Amen.

Pastor's preaching was that we are not powerless. (My husband and I were at church together.) See Acts 1:7–8. These are roadblocks: ignorance, unbelief, and unconfessed sin. You cannot hold on to your sin and expect God to fill you with the Holy Spirit. You cannot hide from God, the storm of love, the impossible. God does the impossible. Rev. Edgar's vision was the pouring love of Christ like a storm showering down as we were praying for our grandchildren just as Niagara Falls. He saw the umbrellas opened, and they were all black, and we came against it in Jesus's name. He also had another vision of me writing a book, a new ministry in marriages.

## Rev. Edgar's Vision

"Moses, those that are with God, come to my side. And those that were against him, the ground swallowed them up." We prayed for our families. God reminded me of his faithfulness. Even when friends and family turned their back on me, God has been faithful to me. My husband turned his back on me, but God never did. He is faithful, faithful, faithful. Amen.

My prayer continued for my family and grandkids and for my son's house and his two cars. I prayed for my husband, which was the same prayer Rev. Edgar prayed.

Rev. Edgar's vision: See the ocean. God destroyed the sin. I see you walking in the ocean, you and your husband. I see you getting married again using a white dress, pure white. "It is done. It is done," says the Lord. I am walking through the sea, and at the end, we have the victory. The ocean closed, took all the sin, and destroyed it. "It is done. It is done," says the Lord. Amen. Rev. Edgar prayed this same prayer I prayed, and as he prayed, the Holy Spirit poured down on him and myself. This was the prayer I prayed for before I called him in the morning, and the Lord poured in his Spirit to pray the same prayer as me without him knowing that I prayed for this.

## Prayer with Rev. Edgar on Love

Love conquers all. The love of Christ covers all multiple sin. I asked the Lord, "What should I pray for my husband?" I heard love. I prayed that morning when I called Rev. Edgar. He started praying for the same prayer, and he began to pray for my husband. The Lord was speaking. "For God so loved the world he gave his only begotten Son."

## Prayer with Rev. Edgar

He started praying, and the Lord told him to be silent and for me to pray, and the Holy Spirit came down upon me. Rev. Edgar got his breakthrough today. Amen. I started crying out to the Lord, "I am ready for my miracle in Jesus's name. God, my husband says he's leaving in June, and I told my husband, 'God is in control.' Lord, you know exactly what's going to happen. I trust you with my marriage, and you are going to make a miracle here, Lord. If it's meant to be or you allow my husband to leave, there is a reason. I see my husband like the prodigal son. I rebuke this in the name of Jesus. You will bring him back. Win my husband, Lord. Win his soul. I pray in the name of Jesus that my husband be delivered in Jesus's name. It is done. You are in control. Yes, Lord."

In church, the pastor preached about true success. (My husband and I were together in church.) You are weak, warm like water. I will spit you out. Success is in spiritual riches. Some people spend so much time on other things that are not of value. Having a personal relationship with the Lord, it's about him, not you. Build your relationship with God in prayer that will last. As I have heard many times, only one life will soon be passed. Only what is done for Christ will last. These things of the world won't last. To be successful is in Christ. You cannot hide from God. See Revelation 19:7–8.

The pastor's preaching was "We are so blind that we don't see our miserable condition. When God gives us a vision, it's not a question of what he does. It's what we do. When we do his way, it's true success. It's not our way. It's his way."

## Word from the Lord through Rev. Edgar

As we prayed, the Lord says, "You're not alone. I am with you." If Christ is in me, who can be against me? No one. He is the author and finisher of my life. Christ is with me. Who can be against me? Thank you, Lord, for your word today. Amen.

We prayed for blessings upon blessings. We prayed for Rev. Edgar receiving a vehicle. He had a vision of a truck in front of his house.

Today is the day of our blessings. You will receive news today. Be ready. Today is the day, not yesterday or tomorrow. Today is the day. Amen. God put in my heart to pray for my husband, not only to sing (which is his gift) but to be a prayer warrior. I prayed for a man that will put God first in everything; a man that will do God's will, not his; a man that prays for all things first and speaks to the Lord; a man that when he starts praying, he falls in love with the Lord more and more; a prayerful man that depends on the Lord and not of the things of this world in Jesus's name. Amen. (The news I received today was a phone call from one of my family members that my mother was admitted to ICU.)

I left on an early morning flight to New York City. During this time, I spent it with my mother in the hospital and my eight other siblings. A very difficult time it was, especially battling with my present situation in my marriage. And I kept quiet of my situation for my mother's sake and my siblings' so that they would not have to worry about me. Aside from all of this, my husband was not supportive of me, and I felt alone.

Good Friday, my mother took her last breath and went home with the Lord. During this period of time was my daughter's birthday that fell on the twenty-third, which I was sad because not once had I been absent on her birthday, and this pained me even more.

My mother's funeral services took place around this time as well, and this was truly heavyhearted for me.

## Prayer and Vision from Rev. Edgar

He started praying for the blood of Jesus to cleanse my house inside and out. There is power in the blood of Jesus. No demon can penetrate through the blood of Jesus. Amen.

In church, there was a speaker. John was weeping and crying, and he had his book and did everything he was supposed to do and was so tired. He closed his book and was fed up because he was too tired and shut his book abruptly, and God said, "Be still."

## Rev. Edgar's Vision

He is closing the chapter of the book of my life. The past is going to be a new book in my life. Jesus said, "No more old. Behold, the old has passed away. All things are new." Amen.

# New Chapter, New Story in My Life

## Prayer with Rev. Edgar

I am complete in Jesus's name. Another prayer was for my daughter Priscilla for a financial breakthrough coming into her life. We also prayed for families. Another prayer was for Rev. Edgar and his wife.

I ask you, Lord, to bless my children and that they seek you continuously. I ask for protection for my grandchildren that they find you soon and be successful in the world and in you, Lord. In Jesus's name, I ask you, Lord, to help me in my job.

## Prayer with Rev. Edgar, a Vision God Gave Him

God is looking down on us with the angels telling them, "Look at these two how they're praying." Today is the day. (Psalm 103 was read.) We prayed to God to break the curse of finances in our lives and our children's lives as well.

I was speaking with my son, Eli, and the word from God was through him, "In order to learn how to win, you got to learn how to lose, and I have the victory. Believe through him in Jesus's name." Rev. Edgar saw the Holy Spirit.

At church, the pastor made an altar call for a refill of the Holy Spirit. He spoke to me, and I went up front, and the Lord spoke to me and said that he is closing the doors that need to be closed. And he is using me for my marriage and for me to try not to understand what's going on. He is going to make a way and bless this marriage more than ever. He is closing the door in this marriage. God spoke to me using the usher, and he is closing the door that needs to be shut.

## Vision from Rev. Edgar

You are going to be blessed. God is with you. He sees me and my daughter Jennifer together. I am not going to be alone. He sees a lot of people around me. He crowned me as queen of God for his plan of salvation. Today we pray to let me know that I am his queen for his plan of salvation. Today I am God's queen for the plan of salvation. Amen. It's God and me. "Never forget this day," says the Lord. Rev. Edgar saw business cards. I am a virtuous woman for the plan of salvation.

## A Prayer and a Vision from Rev. Edgar on Healing

The love of the Lord is going to be a breakthrough in my life soon, as the Lord says. For my daughters, my son, there's a breakthrough in Jesus's name.

There's a breakthrough in Rev. Edgar and his family's life. Thank you, Jesus. Because of the love for us, there is going to be a breakthrough and healing in our lives. The Lord put on Rev. Edgar's heart to call my daughter Priscilla. When I called her, my daughter was crying so much and praying for a miracle. God showed him a vision that she was praying.

I woke up at 5:00 a.m.. The Lord woke me up, and I started praying for salvation for my family. I opened the Bible to Psalms 20, and Rev. Edgar had a vision and a prophecy. He was telling me that I am walking in the promised land, and I'm not going to be alone.

"I will send my Son with you. You are free, and you are walking with my Son, and you're free. I am setting you free. This marriage wasn't good for you. Trust in me. I am setting you free. I am going to guide you. I am preparing you. Walk free and don't look back. I am your promised land, and I am setting you free. No longer are you in your past. You are free from your past," says the Lord. Amen.

Also in this vision, Rev. Edgar stated that I am going to take a trip to Connecticut. I am free today, walking in the light, no more darkness. I am walking with the Lord to the promised land. The Lord is going to take care of me. He will provide, and God is my husband. I am walking out my house, and he's going to move me out of here. He doesn't want me to stay here.

Be ready. Pray and just be ready. Trust the Lord. The past is the past. The past is no longer my life. God is going to take me to the promised land. "Be ready," says the Lord.

Rev. Edgar was praying. The Lord said that I am going to be a shining light in my life. I am going to be that little light, just like Tinker Bell's light out of people's lives, leading people out of darkness into the light.

## Another Prayer with Rev. Edgar

No one like Jesus would die for me. No one like Jesus would die for my husband just to set his spirit free. There is no one like Jesus. I saw darkness, and now I see light. I started singing and seeing light. Only Jesus can set him free. Jesus, you're going to set him free into the light in Jesus's name. Amen. Father, wherever my husband is right now, let my husband be right with you. Breathe on him in Jesus's name. We prayed for Rev. Edgar's daughter, and he saw a beautiful vision of her life in the near future.

We also prayed for my son to get his check that he's waiting for to fix his house. There was a spirit of peace. We prayed and cried from our hearts. God heard our prayers. Rev. Edgar and I prayed for his breakthrough in his finances.

## A Word from the Lord

"I am who I am. Listen to my voice. I will walk with you to the Red Sea. I am going to lead you. Do not fear," says the Lord. "Follow my voice. Listen to my voice only. I am going to take care of you. I am going to supply all your needs. Listen to my voice. I will open the Red Sea and will walk with you in the dry land. So in the midst of it all, I will take care of you." The Lord is my shepherd, and I shall not want (Psalms 23).

I prayed for a breakthrough to break the curse of finances to be broken, and Rev. Edgar saw a white cloud in his home. We prayed and worshipped and gave God the glory. The Lord gave us a verse, Zephaniah 3:17.

We were praying and saying, "Enough is enough. Jesus is fighting our battles." We prayed for our children, and Rev. Edgar saw the angels.

We prayed for the unbelievers in our family to be saved. We prayed for love to pour on our family's lives so that we have a foundation in God's promises.

## Prophecy by Rev. Edgar from the Lord

Rev. Edgar said, "The Lord told me to tell you that everything you wrote in your book, he hasn't forgotten you. He is going to take care of you. As soon as he leaves, the Lord is going to take care of you. Christ is your husband. He made you a virtuous woman. Remember his promise. The Lord sees your pain, but the Son took that pain today. When he leaves you, he knows it's going to be painful. 'Cry out to me,' says the Lord. Stand firm. You're at the end of the storm. You're going to see Jesus at the end of the storm. You're walking over the storm. He's leading you into your new life. Something big is going to happen, and you're coming out of this storm. 'I am going to be with you,' says the Lord. There's victory in your life. I see you coming out of the storm."

He said, "Just pray for him."

And the Lord said that when anyone asks me about my husband to tell them to pray for him and never bash my husband or talk bad about him. God said not to bash anyone because you will not be blessed.

"You and your daughter Jennifer are being blessed with a new home. Something big is going to happen. You are leaving your home. Don't look back because you are going into the new future."

There is peace of tranquility and peace of the spirit of the Lord. We prayed for God to bless Rev. Edgar's missions trip to Honduras. We prayed for the nation and all that is going on. We prayed for healing for our nation. We prayed for my children so that when we get together they can see that God has everything under control in their mother's life.

## A Vision from Rev. Edgar

The Lord is going to speak. Be silent. I am moving out in September, and the Lord showed him a window, and he saw blue water.

Sunday in the hospital with my husband, I was not feeling well and in a lot of pain and pressure in my head on the left side. This was very uncomfortable, and I told the Lord, "I know you are with me, and I trust in you that you are with me."

Rev. Edgar was in my home, and we prayed for my marriage in my home when we prayed and felt a bad spirit in my home. We rebuked it that moment, and God showed Rev. Edgar it was a bad spirit in the corner of my home next to the front door entrance.

As Rev. Edgar and I were praying, there was a spirit of calmness, victory in Jesus's name. The Lord revealed to Rev. Edgar all four of us (my husband, me, Rev. Edgar, and his wife) walking together.

There was a gathering at my home with Rev. Edgar, his wife, my son and his wife and their daughter, and my daughter Jennifer. My daughter-in-law shared a few verses with me:

| | |
|---|---|
| Hebrews 4:12 | Luke 19:20 |
| Isaiah 55-11 | Ephesians 6:10–20 |
| 2 Peter 1:3–11 | 1 Corinthians 13:4–7 |
| John 16:30–33 | James 1:19–27 |
| Romans 8:37 | 2 Corinthians 10: 3 |

This was the day that I shared to all of them what God is doing in my life and how God put in my heart to write a book. Rev. Edgar and I prayed and lifted up our families in prayer. Rev. Edgar and

I prayed for my daughter Jennifer and a dear friend's father-in-law who lives in Kissimmee, Florida. We prayed for Rev. Edgar's missions trip to Honduras. He is faithful. My God is faithful.

Rev. Edgar and I were praying for him to be blessed with a truck. Rev. Edgar saw a vision of his truck. We were praying and proclaiming that in God, all things are possible.

Rev. Edgar and I were praying, and the Lord spoke to Rev. Edgar in prayer telling me to start thinking of putting my book together. Amen.

## A Vision from Rev. Edgar

God has big things for you, so stay focused. He sees me walking outside of my house taking a trip. We prayed for the Lord to heal me and to forget my past. We prayed for my book and prayed for what title to name my book as I had written down several titles.

We prayed this morning before I went to work, and God reminded me to read my book of promises.

The Lord reminded me on this day, Father's Day, that it's the first without my husband. But my Father in heaven is with me. What better Father's Day than to spend it with the Lord? God reminded me he will never leave me nor forsake me. What a great Father's Day, and he will fill me with his love, joy, peace and gives me what I need. He provides for me, and he will give me his promises. Amen. My problem is big, but my God is bigger than my problem. Amen. You don't know what door your marriage is in until God intervenes in your marriage.

## A Vision from Rev. Edgar

"I see an abundance of money coming toward your way. Prepare yourself and be ready for it today, Sule. I see money coming to you. Something big is coming your way."

During this prayer and vision, Rev. Edgar saw my dearest friends who are a married couple praying in their room. Because you've been faithful to the Lord, he will take care of you.

Rev. Edgar, his wife, myself, my daughter, my son and his wife and their daughter, my dear friends and their children all gathered in the hotel room for a birthday celebration. On this day, Rev. Edgar prayed for everyone and prophesied for everyone, and it was a powerful prayer. On this day I prayed to the Lord that I want to have a marriage-conference gathering. Amen. I was meditating with the Lord and asking him, "When will I be getting married again, and when is the restoration for my marriage? When is the day my husband is coming back? I ask you this in Jesus's name so that I could have the best wedding and be prepared and victorious in Jesus's name. I would love to have it in Disney near the castle and with the horse and carriage."

"Taste and see that the Lord is good" (Psalm 34:8).

God put this in my heart to speak on the day of a marriage conference. God said to me, "Try me. Yes, your husband comes home. You have dinner ready. The house is clean." Or it could be the wife coming home from work, and the husband has dinner ready, and the house is clean. God said again, "Try me in your marriage. Put your trust in me. Let me guide you and show you. We need to change." Let God work in us. He will bloom you away like a field of flowers growing that when all has bloomed and grown they need to be cut and trimmed, and that's what keeps it growing. God says, "Try me and see how far you will go with me. I will bless you in your life and marriage."

We need to change. Let go and let God do it. You keep bumping heads with each other. Sometimes God would allow things to happen in your marriage and then he would heal your marriage. "Try me and let me be in you and show you." God's way is better than your way. My way is peaceful, joyful, and patient. With God, love conquers everything.

I was at a training, and I met this lady, and she shared with me how she lost her husband who was murdered, and she also lost her grandson in a car accident. She then began to speak beautiful words to me. I prayed for her, and she prayed for me. And with our situations, we were both able to encourage each other. God was able to show me that we both were not alone.

On this day was a regular routine in my home. I had one of my moments, and I began to cry and asked the Lord, "Why me? Why do I have to go through this?" And I then heard the Lord speak clearly to me, "You are the chosen one, like how my Son was chosen to die for you. You are the chosen one."

God is covering you. I later then watched a Christian TV channel, and the Lord spoke in my spirit, "Where there is no peace, there is no power." The deeper we get with God, the better relationship we have with the Lord. God fights our battles.

Today would have completed nineteen years of marriage.

My return from my trip to Connecticut was where I was able to be there with my family during a difficult time to attend a funeral. (While I was in Connecticut, I got to share my testimony with my family, and they were blessed.) I saw clearly why I had to go out there and how God had a purpose for me. My first prayer back with Rev. Edgar, I prayed that I will be blessed with my own home and my finances and that the home will be paid off.

## Prayer with Rev. Edgar

Break through; God has big plans for you and Jennifer. The waves are big, a tremendous breakthrough in your life, and people are going to know who you are. Great mighty things are coming your way. The Lord God says, "Everything you lost, you are getting back and better. I am blessing you because you put me first and love me more than your husband."

The Lord told me, "You are a blessed woman. You took care of everything." Read Proverbs 31.

You are going to be blessed and highly favored. A vision from Rev. Edgar saw me breaking my mop stick. My future is already done, and he's going to open mighty doors in my life. It is done. Your future is done in Jesus's name. God is putting you favor, and it's coming like a big wave of a tsunami. He said he will show you mighty things, taking your life completely. The blessing of the Lord is coming your way.

I saw on TV of a preacher that said, "God will put that person in your life to pray with you and see the vision." He also stated that that's a story that we can share for God's glory. Your life is coming, and everyone will want to hear your story. This is my moment. What the Lord planted on the ground is going to grow, and the world is going to see it. The seeds are all growing, and the roots are coming out.

Another preacher on TV stated that out of our brokenness is where God's divinity comes out. God looks for brokenness so that the love of God floats in our life and so that God could break the vessel and bring love to our life. (All of these mentioned are all confirmations of what God has been telling me all along.)

The Lord told Rev. Edgar to tell me to prepare myself and get ready to dress the part, look professional, and buy new attire for my journey because he is preparing me.

The preacher in church says, "Some of you are afraid to follow Jesus." You don't need to have a diploma to serve Jesus; anyone and everyone can serve him. Read 1 Corinthians 13:1–4.

Love will never fail. Your love will be elevated. Your love will be motivated.

God, thank you. I am going to exceedingly meet my expectations. He knows exactly what we need. He will line up the right people. God has new expectations in your life. By you being faithful, he is going to take you to places you never dreamed of. Remember your crown. Your story is your gift. When you come out of your story, everything comes with you. We pray for family. Even when I take the bus as my transportation, God favors me.

Today with Rev. Edgar, we also prayed for my situation. There was a prayer for a breakthrough and walking into the promised land to receive our blessings. We started praying for people, and when I was praying, I found a love that I never knew, and that love was the love of Christ.

## Vision by Rev. Edgar

When Mary went forward expecting the birth of Jesus, she was a blessed woman and virtuous woman. The Lord was telling me that

I will go forward, and my life is already written. Being ready to go forward, it was stated to me that I was seen on TV. The anointing of the Lord came down on Rev. Edgar, and he prayed for my book, and it was a powerful prayer.

## TV Network Preaching

Humble yourselves, and he will exalt you. With the anointing of every believer, he will bless you in your business. If he called you to lead people, he will anoint you. When God has called you to do his work, God's anointing, he protects you. He anoints you with the oil of gladness. You are living in acres of diamonds. If you have your wife, you have acres of diamonds. Because if you don't, God will take care of her. He will make her feel pretty and beautiful.

The love of your life can't grow a plant in a plot because it's limited. When roots go down deeper in the ground, it brings stability to grow more. Jesus showed deep love, and some rejected him. We have to show real love. God lead the prayer on this day. He had us pray for the light in us. We need to be brighter. There are some Christians with dim light. Start being brighter. We need light in our lives. I am not angry at my situation. God made me forget all of my toil. God called me to prosper, and I am blessed right now. I am going to be the head and not the tail. I am going to prosper in this moment. The more you value God, the more you are powerful in putting God first in your brokenness. "I know that's why I chose you," says the Lord.

## Rev. Edgar Prophecy

When I was younger and raising my children by myself, I was alone, and God is stepping in right now. What my husband can't give me, God will give me, and I am going to give him everything. The Lord says, "I am not going to suffer anymore."

When my husband abandoned me, God came and bandaged me up. When he left me, God came for me. When my husband stopped loving me, God loved me even more. When he stopped believing in me, God believed more in me. God said that he is going to care for me and my children. My husband came to my life and helped me raise my children when they were teenagers. My husband and I were married for nineteen years, and then he decided to abandon me, and God stepped in to help me. The Lord told me, "Listen and wait on me. Your husband is coming back knocking on your door asking for forgiveness." The only way you pray for someone is through the love of Christ. When God calls you to write, it's not you. It's him.

I was praying quietly in my spirit. The Lord reminded me that thirty-nine years ago I had my firstborn, my son, and I had to have an emergency C-section. My parents, my church, and the pastors were praying for me because I was in a coma and ended up in the ICU. When I woke up a little after a week and I opened my eyes, my vision was blurry, and I couldn't move. My body was aching, and the nurse helped me get out of the bed to start walking again and took me to see my son for the first time. The devil tried to take me then, but I am here by the grace of God. He couldn't take me then and sure cannot take me now! Hallelujah!

I was being attacked spiritually about not arguing about verses in the Bible because the devil wants to divide family. Satan's strategy is to divide us, and he is a liar, and all he wants is to doubt the truth in God's Word. He will misguide you. Where will you stay? Where will you stand? One day we will stand before God, and we will know the truth, and it will be too late. You can't go around with clutter on how they raised you and how you are treated. When you let go, God will prepare a table for you to go forward. He's going to let your enemies see you blessed.

## The Story of Job

When he was attacked, he lost his house. He lost everything. Three of his friends talked bad about him, and God protected him, and God asked the three men to ask Job to pray for them so that God would not bring his wrath upon them. God then gave Job everything that was lost back to him. When they see your book, they are going to ask you for forgiveness. It is done in Jesus's name. Amen. God gave Job seven times more blessings and a new successful life. Forget what happened to you. Bless them and pray for them. I continue praying and thanking the Lord for all he has done in my life. I am going to show you where you are, and now I am going to bless you. Abraham was blessed when he was ninety years old. God is going to bring me to his promised land. God planted a seed in my life, and the enemy is not fighting where I am. He is fighting me in where God is going to take me.

Lord, I don't want you to serve me. I want to serve you. Your tears are going to be healing for someone else. God is preparing you to put you in a platform. We need grace in our lives. We prayed a powerful prayer with Rev. Edgar, and the Lord said to me to rest in peace; the miracle is already done. Praying for my situation, the anointing of the Lord was very strong. The Lord told me to continue to rest in peace; the miracle is done. It is done. It is done. On June 31, my husband left, and on July 26, he filed for the divorce. I was very hurt and told him to not file that date because our anniversary was on July 29. Still during this time, I was trusting in the Lord, and I prayed for God to help me though this emotionally. My Lord was so good to me and had me on a flight on July 29, which again was my anniversary date. I was on that plane praising God and thanking him that I was so close to God, and I was laughing with my Lord even though this was so hard for me because we always would celebrate our anniversary. This was very strange not hearing from one another, but God had me in the palm of his hands.

I felt in my spirit and asked, "Why do people go to work, and they serve at work and get mistreated, yet we are faithful being at work because we need to go and get paid?" The Son died for us, carried our sin, and we stop serving him when things go wrong. We give up, but we still keep being present at our jobs. Our God is faithful, and he loves us, and he wants the best for us. He will provide for us, and we need to please the Lord. We don't need to serve someone that continues to mistreat us. Why be faithful to a job that mistreats you and you don't love it? We continue going to work when we are not happy, serving our duties at work, and we don't love our job. When the Lord died for us on the cross and situations are not going well, we give up. For Christ that did everything for us, we easily get discouraged and stop serving him. You want to see your life turn around and be blessed? Let God lead you. If you trust him, he will bring you out of your bad situation. I am walking by faith and not by sight. He will restore everything back to me and better.

This is the main reason why I have a great relationship with the Lord. I trust him with my life and soul. I lost my mother, and at the same time, I am losing my husband. I practically lost everything. I lost my beautiful apartment on the beach as well.

"'For I know the plans I have for you,' declares the Lord, 'plans to prosper you and not to harm you. Plans to give you hope and a future'" (Jeremiah 29:11). And let your yesterday be yesterday in God. You have both future and hope.

I continue believing and trusting in the Lord. Virtue means doing the right thing. Learn to live your life to please him, our Lord.

On September 11, I was praying with Rev. Edgar, and the Lord was so powerful and moving. Rev. Edgar prayed for my children, my stepson, and entire family.

A word from Rev. Edgar on September 12, he said that the spirit of the living God is in me right now. He loves me today. Forever lasting love breathes on me right now. The Lord told me to breathe deep because he is giving me a new life. Breathe deeply and inhale the spirit of God. Rev. Edgar saw another vision of an airplane with the flight crew that works on the runway seeing him and I on the plane ready to take off. God is saying to keep my eyes and ears attending to his Holy Word. We are going to move forward as he continues to give us the Word. The people in the plane that he saw are the people working for us.

Praying with Rev. Edgar, I began to see a cup overflowing with blessings, pure and white as snow. The Word says, "Let them drink and never be thirsty again." This is over flowing with blessings.

## Vision from Rev. Edgar

I am walking out of the cave like Jesus did. No longer living in the past, I am going forward into the new future, a virtuous woman. Jesus and I are coming out of the cave, walking together hand by hand, and he and I with the white gown. I am glowing all in white with a bright light upon us.

I am virtuous doing the right thing for Christ. Amen.

## My Time Is Coming

I believe in the Lord. My time is coming for my miracle. Today is the word. Nothing is more important. He is faithful, and he is a God of his word. He is powerful. Everyday God is doing something new in my life.

How am I going to break the flow? I am coming back with the anointing. I am coming back with the courage. Elijah came with a lot of wisdom. On September 20, 2019, on a Friday, my son texted me and stated he will be coming by my house to pick up my table, my bed, removing all my personal belongings out of the house. I began to feel deeply pained on what was occurring for me and my situation. I cried so much and talked to the Lord and expressed to him how I felt. This was a terrible feeling and knowing that I will not have a home anymore and I am losing everything. I cried out so loud and told the Lord, "I trust you and know you have something bigger and better for me!" As I walked out of my apartment for a brief moment, there was a strong wind, and I heard the Lord tell me, "You hear the wind moving fast? That's how fast and big your blessing is coming."

Waiting on God is hard, but God keeps his promises. My season is coming, and I am not giving up. This is a season, not a sentence. God is giving me the ending to this book. As with the vision from Rev. Edgar, he has already opened the Red Sea, walking right into the promised land. Victory over my life, we are champions in Jesus's name. My home is coming. When Moses was with the people, God said, "What do you have in your hand?" Moses feeling scared at the sea and not sure on what to do next, the Lord reminded him again on what he had in his hand. Then the Lord opened the Red Sea. This is the same way the Lord is blessing me in my situation and reminded me that I am walking in the Red Sea to the promised land. God then told me as he said to Moses, "What do you have in your hand?" The Lord placed in my spirit, "Rest in peace." I will be like a fast train, and no one will be able to stop me. I am blessed with God's anointing. I am the captain of the train with Jesus, and he is in front of me, beside me, and behind me.

## Prayer from Rev. Edgar

God created the world in six days. My situation is so small to the Lord, and he can change it around in seconds. Feeling down, I prayed with Rev. Edgar, and God came for a breakthrough for me. God showed Edgar this vision of Jesus and me walking through the Red Sea to the promised land moving forward. What you thought was the end is the beginning. I am walking through this valley, and I am going to push through the mountain. The reason why we don't see the mountain tall is because we quit in the middle of the valley. Your praise is getting you ready for your next level. I close this chapter with tears because I am going to my next chapter with new life and a new praise. Amen.

I began to pray for all my family members and those in need. You know who they are, Lord, and I want to tell you that through all of this situation, even in my brokenness, I've learned to have an awesome relationship with you, Lord, and how you blessed me big even in the small things. God, I love you to eternity, Lord.

November 1, I checked my mail and opened it, and it was my final divorce papers. Here I am trying to forget all of it, but it was very hard to see it and read the fine print. I am walking through this valley, but I am not giving up. Lord, I trust you with all my heart. I go through my emotions and my moments in my marriage. I felt so neglected, lonely, unpretty, and felt worthless. I felt I wasn't good enough, but when I spoke to God, "I don't know what to do here," all I began to do thereafter was spend more time with the Lord from morning to night and began to pray my way out of it.

God reminded me that he loves me and he is with me and freed me even when I went to court. My Letter to My Husband

As I was sitting in court, I wrote a letter to my husband what the Lord placed in my heart, and it was not easy.

I wrote to him that this was not going to be easy for us. "God loves you and that my children love you. My grandkids love you."

I wrote to him that I always pray for him and send my blessings to him. "If you need me, I'm here. Take care. And this is the last time I can say, 'from your wife.'"

And the judge looked me straight in the eye and told me, "I am free." This was God reminding me that I am free. Even when I wanted to give up, I wouldn't because God is faithful to me like no man can. The love of Christ is so strong and so pure. I will put my hope in God, and I will praise him again and again, my Savior. But if anyone suffers as a Christian, let him not be ashamed. Let him glorify God.

## Rev. Edgar Prophecy

The Lord is telling you that when you walk out of the cave, you will have all of the miracles in your life. When he tells you to take that first step, don't be afraid. When Jesus came out of the cave, he took that first step and did more when he walked out of the cave than when he was alive. The Lord said, "Be still and know I am the Lord." When Jesus Christ was on the cross and gave his spirit, it is done. The Lord reminded me that it is done and told me that he will continue to take care of me. Now I began to get in my emotions, and the holidays were getting closer. It only became difficult for me as this was the first year without my husband. However, I reminded myself that it would be okay as I would be spending it with my children. Praying with Rev. Edgar, God reminded me about when he carried the cross and how he still then did not give up. I won't give up. I will keep believing. As I got ready for work that day, Rev. Edgar prayed that someone today will give me a word of encouragement.

A lady approached me this day and just shared with me to not let the makeup she was wearing fool me. She shared that she had been through tough times, slept in her car, worked different jobs with no stability, but she kept going to church and raising her hands. No one knew what she was going through and told me that God would be taking me out of my situation and that he was going to burst me out of it. And when people read my story, they are going to be blessed. She then proceeded to tell me that where God is taking me, no man can stop me. I was so overwhelmed in the spirit, and this was all confirmation from the Lord. I did not know this lady, and she did not know me, but I received it because I knew it was from the Lord.

Praying with Rev. Edgar, the Lord reminded us to feed his sheep. If you love me, feed my sheep. I was praying a powerful prayer, and the Lord answered my prayers and told me to have fun in New York City with my daughter and family and that he was going to use me out there. I will be fasting for my daughter out there, my new home, and my new book. Praying and fasting for my other daughter and my son, leaving all in God's hands.

I was in church, and the pastor's preaching was titled "What Is the Best Bread?"

A woman came to me and told me she doesn't know what I am going through, but the Lord is telling her to tell me that whatever I am going through, God will bring me through it. And the testimony will be greater than what it is right now, and God has me in the palm of his hand. And who you are constantly praying for, God has not forgotten your prayer. Do not look what is around you. When the devil tries to remind you of it, you tell the devil that God has you in the palm of your hand.

Rev. Edgar was praying with me, reminding me that I am God's queen, and as soon as I leave for my flight, God is going to talk to me on the plane and use me. God used me, and I spoke to a lady on the plane where she was sitting on the opposite side of me and then ended up on the side of me, and I then began to witness to her. God will use me for his plan out there in Connecticut. When I was out there, I shared my story to several ladies, and the Lord told me to tell them to put him first and to please him.

In prayer, God told me in 2019 to begin to walk into 2020 and rest peacefully. On Christmas Day was my flight out to New York City, and in one of my prayers, I heard the Lord asking me about the most out of my trip that I want. I told the Lord that I want to be at Rockefeller and see the big Christmas tree and spend it with the Lord. God made it happen. I was so excited, and arriving to the hotel, I had a great view with a huge window, and across the street was the ball drop on the rooftop with the big screen TV in front of the ball drop. I kept thanking God for everything and making all this happen for me. In the beginning, God always reminded me that he will take care of me and that he is real. On Friday, January 10, the Lord had Rev. Edgar pray for me and anoint me. God said that he is going to use me to speak to the ladies and not to be afraid and that he loves me for being obedient, and I spoke from my heart.

I spoke from my heart with God leading me, and I began to share my testimony with the ladies who then began to feel blessed by hearing what God was doing in my life and continue to do. So don't forget that where God is taking you, no man can stop it. And remember that the reason why I follow Christ and trust in him is because he is my healer, provider, my life. He is Lord, holy, the first and the last, our Savior, God, joy, wisdom of the wise. He will never leave you nor forsake you. When you fall, he lifts you up. When you are broken, he mends you. And when we feel death, he takes us home with him. In order for you to shine, you have to break like a glow stick. In order for you to see that stick glow, you have to break it. And when you see it, it's a beautiful color of God's creation. Amen.

## Vision from Rev. Edgar

I was going through my storm, and now I have grown strong in the Lord. People are going to know about you and love you. I am going forward.

Now to my readers, I leave you with this question: What happens when God chooses you?

# About the Author

S he is a new author in this industry and wanting to share her testimony with the world. She is a Latin American, born in Puerto Rico and the sibling of ten and a mother of three.